A Camouflage of Specimens and Garments

Also by Jennifer Militello

Anchor Chain, Open Sail (chapbook)

Flinch of Song

Body Thesaurus

A
CAMOUFLAGE
of
SPECIMENS
and
GARMENTS

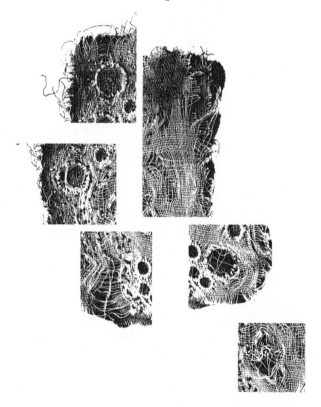

JENNIFER MILITELLO

T|P

TUPELO PRESS
NORTH ADAMS, MASSACHUSETTS

Library of Congress Cataloging-in-Publication Data available upon request.
ISBN: 978-1-936797-75-2

Cover and text designed by Bill Kuch.
Cover: "Little Stitches" (2014) by Julia Wright. Rust-dyed fiber
with freeform embroidery. Used courtesy of the artist
(www.juliawright.co.uk).

First paperback edition: May 2016.

The epigraph is from *A Certain Lucas* by Julio Cortázar (Knopf, 1984).
Used with permission of Carmen Balcells Agencia Literaria S.A., Penguin
Random House, and translator Gregory Rabassa.

Tupelo Press
P.O. Box 1767, North Adams, Massachusetts 01247
Telephone: (413) 664–9611
editor@tupelopress.org / www.tupelopress.org

Tupelo Press is an award-winning independent literary press that
publishes fine fiction, nonfiction, and poetry in books that are a joy to
hold as well as read. Tupelo Press is a registered 501(c)(3) nonprofit
organization, and we rely on public support to carry out our mission
of publishing extraordinary work that may be outside the realm of the
large commercial publishers. Financial donations are welcome and
are tax deductible.

for Dylan and Fiona

CONTENTS

Now that he's growing old he realizes that it's not easy to kill it.

It's easy being a hydra but killing it isn't, because if it's really necessary to kill the hydra by cutting off its several heads . . . at least one has to be left, because the hydra is Lucas himself and what he'd like to do is get out of the hydra but stay in Lucas . . .

—Julio Cortázar, *A Certain Lucas*

Dear B,

Two months of spasms and still I am not well. Awake is more knives than I can count. I was the one who shut the window. But all the dead flies had already come in. All I remember already got out. You are not the proximity I wait for. You are not real. I am small, but need to be watched. Have I told you a thunderstorm is like getting a million letters from you? Only better. Only more like beginning, not ending, in rain. Today, the cold is beating down the bats from their wings. What I say isn't even close to what I think. It is much worse. Anguish grows gray as it waits in my throat. Like just before snow, when I can smell the holding back.

Song of Interrogation

Not about me.
Not about the wheels as they corrode from their rotors.
Not about the weather or the axis it dregs.
Not about this or that or anything either.
Nothing like a litmus.
Nothing about bliss.
Not a window.
Not a fix.
Not about rain.
Not about bearing witness.
Not about reason or the ways we resist.
Not quite foreign.
Not quite missed.
Not reproducing with the DNA of animals.
Not reproducing.
No replication, wide abyss.
No event horizon or location where chaos begins.
No tiny history.
No flag above a run-down shack.
No pairing of a fork and knife.
Not about scenery.
Not about risk.
Not about the torso or limbs.
Not asking.
Not putting forth answers.
Not plucked like fruit.
Not left like seeds.
Not furrowed or amiss.
Not kissed by the language of skin.
Not existing or lacking.
Not is.
Just maybe a garden.
Just maybe begins.
About without.
About within.
Not about me or the breaking I live.

A Dictionary of the Garment

It came to me without warning.
It came to me coated with wax.
It came to me threaded with silk.
It came to me in wolf's clothing.

It was like a crown that claimed my land.
Like sand, it slipped through the fingers.

It lasts like a pack of dogs.
It barks the gods to madness,
it fraternizes with beasts,
it sniffs the precious scenery from the stars.
It is more tropical than the godless should be.
It is excellent/contagious with gardens.

It has the blood's tiny fires and it stokes them
into the face absence has been blossoming.
It would parade itself before the world.
It has the whistle of a young boy walking the fields.

It was fitted with agitation and a hippocampus:
it would kneel before those overthrown.
It would moan like trees in rain.
An epiphany. A flourish. An axis overdone.

In my isolation, I could not get it to form.
The clay was wrong. The stakes were low.
I moaned too much. There was a beauty like the world.

I felt my own charm.
I felt myself go tin.
I felt myself listen at the keyhole
for whatever in the room was whispering.

Winds cried out. I had doubt as my dark.
I had harps strung with barbed wire. I had pyres
to burn the living since winter is for the dead.

It ends here at the autopsy. A Pentecost fossilized like snow.
A mere sleeve rolled up to expose the arm,
shot through with muscle and light's ferned bruise,
shot through with the grip and its steady alarm.

A Dictionary at the Periphery

On the day I was born, the moon's phase
was waning crescent. No death
to sweeten like a side dish. No infant

to ease from its roughhewn crib and lay
among the savage rushes. No soft words. No
mouth to feed. No rope to hang from. No barn

to raze. The shock of me was an utter root,
cruel in parts, gone as a body, vacuous and
black. Left bankrupt by the witnessing

I'd done, I made a fist and shook it
toward the world. Often blighted. Often
cold. Jagged, late, matted with moons,

aping a gray aroma of flesh, eyeteeth
of a she-wolf, urn of human ash.
A torn god, sad as seasons. Burnt offerings,

poured libations: the remedies I invented
were decanted with abyss. Tongues to mourn
wonder with. A flex like heaven's wings

to lash me to the mast, unmask me,
cradle me to sleep. The day I was made,
I was made veiled. Knee-deep in eucalyptus.

I was made scarved. To understand my wax
and wane, the hint of a sword mood stitching
in my breath, give me a heart of wastelands

or dirt. Eyes mutiny, bland mysteries
of anisette, hunting the char lodged within me.
Things drop stinking into beasts.

One cannot wilt. One shall not want.
I was the last animal at the lamp the night
man was born. Record me in the morgue's lost books.

A Dictionary of Having Been Prey in the Voice of the Grandmother

Replaced by stones in the sewn belly, I could finally be the beast.

Up from the bed I could finally be and the woods were a taste
gracing lichen and teeth and I had the raw aesthetic of deadness
and meat. Finally, I had the limbs it took to recover me.

Split from the belly I was at last and the housecoat had a language
like breath and my life was a theft of something like me
but not like me. The child was not the scar of me, was not meek,

I had been eaten, I was the beast. I had the taste of bewildered flesh,

I had been puppeted by my undone death, I was a sentiment of rebirth.
I had a continent of the canine teeth and the lolling tongue and
of the digestive tract. The bitter juices that licked me whole.

I had an old sense of the precise in me. Kicking its way
to nurse me back. The woodsman had a body like breath
and a deft axe and I was the one by the arm he pulled out,

new with a float of the row toward death, the end about me.

The child with wide eyes had believed. The housecoat had soothed
like a breeze her soft eyes and the fierce wolf had crossbred
deception with all he could eat. The woodsman, the hunter,

one reptile lick since what is a skin but the fair want inside,
the saunter that comes with forgetting the need,
since what is the eye but its syphilis haunt, as the pupil

grew wide (to be at the throat) and narrowed with desire

the folded hands and the tidy sewn quilts and the quaint
kitchens, and I was but a sullen knit suckled at the hum and grip,
mother to the dark rehearsal, I was only a version or test.

I went back from the path through the woods, back to a girl
I hardly knew, though I moved her hands and said her words,
and in my stead a desire to be, beast and not beast, as neither can last

beyond the feed. A nestling of stones in my lone robe of flesh.

A Dictionary of Preserving the Hydrangea's Bloom

First, soften its thousand grand catastrophes of smoke,
small-fisted exotics, unaware of death. Startle the petals'
parchment paper, all in grays beneath the flesh,

scents that have been pinched and rounded, planted down
the hurricane loam, equal parts peat, leaf mold, senile
elegies, lime-free grit. At the center of the hand,

a map for each is pinned. Gestation weeps
more acidity for each deciduous bruise, suggesting
understanding beyond the human crush. Bend

the panicle until it splits, glitters, lords over
the grasp of the stem's relenting vine. Splinter the iris's
dimness, a fine gauze between contrasting eyes. Flay

of the seedless, swimless flutter, lord of the smolder,
the yellow sky's mouths. The last sad vendor
of the intricate's decline. Cover flat with glass and wait.

Architecture: the last occupants, sorrows that are picked,
with fertile or perfect florets, bottles containing poison,
notched, so as to be detected in the dark, by touch.

A Dictionary of the Symphony in the Voice of Ludwig van Beethoven

It's dark and it comes/it's dark and it comes/it's dark and it comes and it's dark

It comes and it's dark and it comes a man on a horse and a falter in a cry and violins in the trees sequins of dresses and in the clouds it's dark it comes tasseled curtains and folded with seams

It comes it walks a bridge of skulls it wears a look it sees for miles it walks and walks it's dark it comes I can smell it I can fight it God

It's dark and it comes it's dark and it's dark it is the surface of a statue absent of limbs and the angels of coffins angels found at the mouths of graves and the men who curl soot from the root of a floor

It's dark and it will fling you over its shoulder tarnish you turn you into a schoolboy harness you the pages of it will random and fly up and its lion will fix on your sleeping face and its animal will cry at the entrance to your yard a house of cards and a stop of clocks a wing and drink of dry

It will marry you whether you accept or not it will enter your scream at the edge of the wood it will enter your color your sunset your mar it will hang as trousers do in noon's closet

You can see it if you peek into the lidlessness of flies into the filing cabinets and ashcans and books you can see it if you close your eyes you can see it if you balance or wind your features in a sheet

Close your eyes and you can see it death of mothers the mildew room

Close your eyes and it will court you run as fast as you can and it will catch you turn the present inside out illness hours occupants remodeled all of it will smoke you out

There is no closing its wound when it is a mouth and keeps you breathing with your wide throat inspired by all that dark the mark of a lack's hand already upon you your green grave waiting your marriage to the flesh

A Dictionary with Foresight as 20/20

Dressed with a self that cannot last, I break
the bread of the moment. Every borrowed body
is a church whose faithful fast. And in my most
ambiguous hours, I dream a storm of scarlet gods

and vestments made from prayer. As daylight takes
my pulse, as the flocks of me are ghosts, death
blossoms like a blown grenade deep in the valves
of my blood. Cries like wine in the wine-red ending:

what I thought were Bibles are my bones.
When I was young, there was dusk in my hair.
I was sultry like the animals. Days became stones
I swallowed to remember. I marked the eye's

promiscuity. There was a great tonight waking
in the womb of the world. Days were
half-filled baskets left along a river's flank
or moved like sonatas through melancholy rooms,

fled windswept roads, fled catacombs as
echolocation, restructured modes of sleep.
My heart filled with villanelles of longing
raised its lost white sail: *now let me*

be still. Let me eat my fill and hunger.
Let such quarantines be declared. My heart
is starched by the emptying streets:
tomorrows want to sleep in my eye.

But I am no host for parasites. I am not
the symbiotic kind. I want to cut my teeth
on the meekness of my ancestors, on the immaculate
lament that is housed inside my throat.

Not one note describes my torso. Not one cry
undoes my oath. I am nothing but a fistful.
A temporary me. Antithesis to survival.
A mere notion: I knew this from birth.

A Dictionary of Venery in the Voice of Artemis

Little birds like a purr garlanding the underbrush.
The little black heart of me cool and dim. The little black daring
of something within. An offseason, a tender centerpiece

of roots. Its beyond stays fetal in the chest.
How many beasts downwind. I step into
the wolf's skin. I howl from its throat, I let

a shadow or sigh gallop the landscape of my hand.
Far off, I haunt my frosted version of the field.
No noise. No muscle twitch. Even the veins licked clean

of their tick. The banks of the river ladder down
toward the river's picked-over bones. A hem of twilight
x-ing in, its hourglass, its stratum of snow.

Dusk's hung kimono coming down. Its silken asides
like brides left at the altar. Its nocturnal blossoms
cry the birds. Disturbed at last by the barge of the moon

as it crosses the burning water. Clouds pass, rabbit pelts.
I lie low, bright with borrowed blood. I smell the wild
in what I kill. Ending suckles at the cloth of birth.

A Dictionary of Faith

Like wind, God eavesdropped in the doorway.
His hybrid anatomy broken. His structured body loose.

God flew, as the last small moths of his lungs and larynx
gave like willows in a basket filled with red birds

where once there were dozens of roses.
As it rained, God's every dry eye trembled.

The moon's fronds of empty grew tentative then,
like what stands in for reason when reason is maimed.

An epidemic of eyes, God flew like a surge collapsing,
divided in the listening like a simple skein of wheat.

His most ferocious hounds were fettered,
predators sheltered in the henhouse of the heart.

A Dictionary of Following and Fading
in the Voice of Eurydice

Stop. My heart dies in the air.
I walk with gray in the lining of my coat,
with my eye set dead in the eye of dusk;
I meet myself mirrored in the wind.

Lily as I am, a mistake named me at birth.
I return to where evening is a foliage.
Its rivers find me weighing my shadow
against their solemn waters. Black trance

where I become an atlas with all its maps
returning. I sing the inevitable vanish beginning.
The object of me flown from the roost,
raven carrying away the shining in its mouth.

Away, clouds. Away this yellow kind of rapture.
My shadow, that lowly dragger of baskets,
a last attempt to sleeve one's lamp,
the paths of which are edged with wheat.

Each of its sutures a crucible in which
reality is tamed. With all its contents
falsely locked. Abbeys ruined and
scarved archaic. A frail pantoum of sleep.

The night as a makeshift garment of wants,
one gray chill in the chambers of loss:
the leverage of empty lifts me up.
The moon's sad ventriloquist of plumage.

A Gospel of the Human Condition

And we are left on the cold sills of a world.
Years come and loiter in the bottles
we discard, years come and stir
with the wind, years singe like cigarettes
as they burn past their filters, the papers
of winter as they ladder to the ground.

Even here, in this mechanical hour,
dying becomes a hundred armored lords.
A grain of sand wears a volt of thought
more soft than the green of torture.
An asymmetry of irises.
The stars, that bed of nails.

It is the howl we make instead of love,
while the pigeons stir their ragged sleep
and sleep their dirty rivers, while
the evening is a crier of wounds.
Hewn, we are the minnows. Shallows
hold us in the bare of our shadows.

Alone, we are mourned by
our own ruined shrines, and the voyages
mine through our waking. What takes, what
makes scalpels of each of the eyes, each
a called mile, each a spun-sharp waiting.
We are faithless, fainting, praying.

The hair shirt is not enough. The fish hook
is not enough. We kiss in the corners
of subway stations. We undress in public.
We are cruel to animals. When we sing,
we sing poorly. Some mechanism in our hearts
fails and this causes a tinkering of happiness.

The old laws take hold. The single hoof
of each of our hearts remains unshod.
Our half-starved dogs are beaten, their ribs
listen to the darkened apartments within,
our voices trim the windows. We are

sure to be forgiven. We are sure to
feast. We oxidize in several winds.
There is shrapnel in the rain. We fade
like several finches. Ourselves
at the periphery. Begotten, not made.

Dear B,

Today, the rain is a dream of wicker baskets. Those dogs in the courtyard who belong to no one keep keeping me awake. The seagulls crying tin cans open. I am not a needle to breed things shut. Soon: isn't that a kind of sleep, layers of cells, how deeply they remain. All I remember now is a child crying at the far side of the road. How, at a touch of morning, the ships grew white as if they were the bones of the drowned. God, B, the rain now. As if lions lie in the circulatory system, the color of sassafras, homesick for the plains. The blood's rooms of anxiety. The drug the need was made for cannot satisfy the need. Now I realize I was made for this half-consecrated world with its one hand running a comb through the stars.

Dear B,

And my letter to you, B, is what blooms fish-silver where I have no heart. Light falls daily as if to swarm. My letter to you is so many places without water and bread. I am sparse these days and my clothes don't fit. I am mildewed and nomadic. Stagnant water at the curb has been breeding in my chest. The world that will live in my fingers. All I know to hold onto slips. A stitched thread to control each buttonhole's abyss. I remember such hospitalizations. I remember thinking God would take me back.

Dear B,

The revision of need in the palm of my hand sings. Is bloated. Must be netted first. Its slow clay a pale slowness I ignore. My fingers touched with a tiny care. The delivery of here like the imagining of there. I take need by the scruff, not to punish it but to make it beg, to transform it into a gutter it already is. A masterpiece. Thin. A paper imperfection. It ends up with an ability to read my veins. I am weakened by its taint. Have control so long it flares like steam. I have control. Snared. Rabid. In my hand, a crowd of needs. It multiplies and shapes me sick. It licks me good. I am a seed, pull moisture from the broad frond earth. The revision is a paradise one. It leaves me loose. It leaves me fall in love. I wish to sing. I must be netted first.

Corrosion Therapy

You're invited. To a crime that, like me
and mine, recalibrates x and y. Misshapen,
the only haven is a knife whose edge is left
unsharpened. All the twisted syncope
of murders is alive. You'll survive
if you stay inside, crack the panes,
imagine the hive of more than one mind
multiplied here. You can thrive. Simply
cut yourself off from you, say your
good-byes, come to our side, your harem,
your tribe, come in and feel at home.
The elevator you ride from the lobby
takes you right to the hazards we hide.
You can't deny your decisions now that
you can smell what we've been, our
living, our pride, our cool little eyes
like rainfall that don't care one bit.
It's suicide only to one part of you.
The other part connives to come, to kick
the lame dog, to take advantage
of the dark, to test the door to alive. Is
it locked or ajar? How far will it open?
If I fit through, who will die? Say
good-bye. Your self was a bore. Your
self was a nun, garrote as her rosary.
You can hear yourself cry in her bare little
room, you can hear what she desires. I won't
give you another chance. I won't tell you
again to confide. Take the letters in
your name and spell it out backwards.
Please its jester by blessing the deep.
The horror of its crack and whip. Take
the future as your wife. Spell the places
that bite, places from which you derive.
You must live with what you fail to cage.
Let you and what you could be collide.

Criminal How-To

Should pick the lock. Should steal the car.
Should crash the car and then drive off.
Should sell the drug. Should do the drug.
Should pilfer from the basket passed around
at church. Should not look the loved one
in the eye. Should drink too much. Should
cough all night. Should trim the fingernails
too short. Should poison the wife. Should
ignite the house. Should shatter the window.
Should err. Should scorn remorse.
Should chat during the funeral. Should
talk and talk. Should fritter away
an adolescence. Should step on the spider.
Should tear the web. Should steal eggs
from the tended nest. Should
carefully weave of the world
a weapon. Should embroider half-truths.
Should plunder. Should pillage. Should fall
short. Should sew laundered money into your
shirts. Should board the bus without a ticket.
Should cross the yellow line. Should case
the joint. Should grow old. Should scoff at
time spent in jail. Should run up debt.
Should remain unemployed. Should leave
your husband. Should want. Should not
want. Should suffocate there in your own
silk sheets. Should feel the highway alive
in your body, as it thins like blood in
your veins. Should escape. Should render
the present a wreck. Should slash
the tires. Should cheat on the test.
Should gas the enemy. Should shun
pleasantries. Should pilfer the flawless
gem. Should smash the eyewear

of the weak. Should mumble promises.
Should let them break. Should call today
a remedy. Should refuse to flaunt. Should
take anything you can. Should lie
in wait. Should walk the streets late
at night. Should spit. Should chew gum.
Should litter. Should take the last portion
left on the plate. Should not make the grade.
Should blunder. Should let the yawn
inside proliferate. Nothing has ever been
this easy. The will to live misplaced.

A Dictionary of Wooing and Deception
in the Voice of the Sociopath

It takes so long to go bad, here in this glad world.
If I loom, what I hate holes up inside me.
I feel where it is broken like a rib. I feel

where it fibs in order to be related.
It follows me home, nose to the scent.
The cat in me is scratching at my tongue.

Let in, it will win you over. Let go and you will
feel yourself grow older as the knives in me
describe the knives you know.

Godless, I am most real. Healed, I am
most ill. Filth is my most honest hour.
The eye of me contains all I am loosely.

The eye of me is hardly mine. It is
a gallery for the overripe. It invents
our lives from five dimensions. Unlike the heart,

its crowbars pry. I am not I.
I barter with the periphery. It is the puncture
in me that mouths the translation.

What I read in the entrails. What the blood reds
become. My eye contains an afternoon.
Its dry mouth made of autumn. I lick at

my wounds. I never cool. I have become
the evidence, I have become degrees. The teams
of horses set loose are my silence. What tension

threads itself like nectar from my wounds.
A man is a house of cards. A man
like a jar, filling slowly. Like wire, like

a vial of warmth. My blood has been sleet
the way it falls in winter. Onto the canvas
as two mediums at once.

A Dictionary of What Can Be Learned in the Voice of the Sociopath's Lover

Recklessness spurred by our limited time,
that they could take nothing from you
if all you had was the wild. To like
too much speed between the trees after dark.
To survive while passing on the narrow bridge,
while kissing without caring less, while
laughing when the cruelty hit. To climb
even though the high was made to collapse,
to bite so deep the seasons bled, to make
enemies who loved me and make criminals
my friends. To wreck whatever touched my hand
to prove I still exist. To not feel guilt.
That nothing matters and nothing will.
To break glass and not get cut, to lie
in a field and not look up. Not to want.
To cut my knee deep and pack sand
into the wound if I was drunk and loved
the sound of the ocean. To haggle
with summer. That nouns were fickle.
That the best note was wrong done,
that when sung it would crash like an engine.
That age was merely come what may.
To race my own incessant heart. To race
the marred world with a quick wit
and a passive face. To bark up
its tree. To fight and spit. To
let it go. To earn my keep.

Conspiracy to Commit Larceny: A Recipe

Take the man you think you love and his
fabulous lips. Take him from one place
to the next. Let him drive your car. Let him
drive it through the mood-crazed woods
until it overheats. Let the nights feed
from your eyes as you look at him. Do
not turn on the heat. Do not spill
the flavored oils of the heart. Do not
eat from the palm of your hand
a fluid ounce of what you need. Do
something illegal. You only have to be there
when they bring the contraband in.
You only have to leave yourself behind.
The stars know. The police will prowl
your neighborhood until the plate number
matches and the car checks out.
When they bring you in, you
must remove your shoes and belt.
You must pretend there was no felony.
Then you must confess. Add your past,
a pinch of the rage you feel, and how
you sit until your father bursts in
and asks whether you have been arrested.
Add a mother who tells you she is
ashamed. An expensive lawyer. The way
you remember the taste of his kiss and
how real he was and how he would
drive dark roads at high speeds through
the back woods with the headlights off.
Remember what the stars see. And how,
once it is over, the lawyer will send
a letter saying he said you knew nothing,
saying he tried to keep you out of it,
though the police said he had given
you up as they made you say his name.

Conspiracy to Commit Larceny

She she she—at the crux of what hurts—(the police came)—thin hospital
sheets—(the air in my lungs exhaling)—(their flashlights searched along
the dirt for the criminal)—(I was up against the car)—(they were gathering
my glances)—the hospital room and her unclean body—(they were
collecting my wildflower looks)—my memories as I said them—(in my
mouth)—(their voices without bodies)—legs could not support her
weight—(I was the criminal)—(they said as much)—what she perceived—
(the darkness of woods and a small circle of headlights)—she reached for
me—she told me they had left her outside the hospital doors—(I am all by
myself)—I pull her socks from her feet—her feet are stones—my temples
throb—(the policeman hears them)—(he puts me in a cell)—(he puts me
behind the thick glass)—(he carves my name into the ink)—(he carves my
name toward the hospital's room)—the nurses turn her body to clean her
after she vomits—her pale thigh—her marbled skin—her inability—(I am
handcuffed)—(my fingertips are stained with ink)—(I have my identity)—
the hallway smells like trying to keep alive—this geriatric wing—unfolds
from my body like a—(flashlight dying)—bulb drifting—(false battery)—
the window out to the river—a slowing barge—(I dream of guilt)—(they
take my shoes)—(they take my belt)—she takes my hand and tells me—
speak—(I sign the paper that speaks for me)—(they read me my rights)—
(they speak for me)—a sad green room—I see myself in the mirror—(they
see me in from the other side of me)—(they read me the law)—as I read
she sleeps—as I read I feed her something that makes her sick—(I roll from
bed)—the thin sheets—the bulletproof river—(its bulletproof glass)—(my
voice buttoned to one side of it)—she reads my look—I tell her—(the
policeman takes my arm and makes me) look—criminal—and finds my
wound and touches it—tests it with an open flame—it changes color in
me—it is not mine—she is waiting—her feet are cold no matter what I
do—and bloodless—(this place is unable to reason)—(unstained)—I rest
my eyes—I am surrounded—(there is nowhere that is not this scene)—
last glance at days that end—(they put me in the car)—(they call in my
name)—her name above the bed is ending as I speak—I carve my name
into the scene—(my hospital is not believing)—is my hope—my heart
stopping when I see the moments—(the policemen say what I mean)—
(and I am clean)—(despite the act)—(the theft)—the rain—(the last
attachment they make to me)—(guilt)—in a world betrayed—by flesh—

A Dictionary of Mechanics, Memory, and Skin
in the Voice of Marion Parker

The world is a wind I thought I heard just before
I heard nothing. The world is what the pulse of me
whispered just before it stalled. A lullaby
I drugged myself with while my slit throat emptied.

If I had risen the casual distance,
if I had run, if I had resisted like metal
not fired enough—but I can end if one man
asks it of me. Already my sewn eyes

are widows, delicate and desolate, a sabotage
in wails. Every direction in me is south. Every
sleep the deception of sleeping. Every corrosion
another part drought. I prefer to fail. I prefer

to be in pieces. No one expects from me now.
No mourning the model specimen, little Marion,
for what she was. The thin room of my animal's
whimper keeps night from the garden.

My limbs have their own dementia, decomposing
like a bloom. Fathers do not hesitate to collect
my rough bones. I will build a womb bathtub-cold
and be born, white as its porcelain, prone. I will

grow old in the minutes it takes to be dismembered:
one suture for each of my antiseptic mouths.
Tattered is how I began. It pleases me to rest among
the lilies though their bulbs long ago burned out.

A Letter to the Coroner in the Voice of Marion Parker

Lay me out as if the coffin is only a dress
or a wedding I never made it to. My God, I will
run off. My family will wait and I will be free
with my hair let down and I will not return.

I do not exist. I know where I belong.
I grow like roots to slow the going open,
to suffocate a moment's recent act,
removing the bloodlike gloves it leaves.

Once inside me, the seasons go arid, the seasons
go mad, they complain of brambles. The crumble
of the mud earth sings, forms rot with a sweetness
breathing. Hours are our daily bread.

There is not a cartridge for all the darkness
I feel. My face is there, a molecule, a shiver
filled with June. I have clarity. I imagine
the shatter is a shatter that stays.

I am trying not to break. Debris is all I am.
My face gaunt where once it was seamless, entrails
replaced by rags, eyelids wired open, a congregation
in my eyes with all the candles held by children.

Come. The bleed of night
has an animal skin. There is livestock
in our hearts. How the dark sticks.
How the damp animal rakes before us.

A Dictionary of Keeping Quiet between the Monstrous and Holy in the Voice of Marion Parker

Surrounded by water, I was not a martyr.
I had collared an engine in myself until I could
go on. Indented and without precedent, I stood
deprived of force. I admitted to a resurrection.
My words were like a pulse.
                              I photographed the end
to justify the means. I found excellence in harmonies
I imagined as remorse. The one citadel mothers me:
I am a battlefed creature. I am miraculous with need.
I am a pair of structures: one puncture and its inception: ✓
one sentence and its creed.
                              My childhood noose
hangs empty. My lampshine a bitter sap that bleeds.
There is a trace of the location in me.
The witch in me is habitual, slit like a throat,   ~vastly
vulnerable in this cold season, punctual in such light.
I am a god. I am alone.   } opposite
                              I am a people. I am gone numb.
I cannot fire the stoves of my eyes, I cannot
collect my nameless organs. I cannot call myself
good. My shadow has the shape of a shadow.
My voice has entire seas. I cannot be made
natural since my flesh
                              burns with these machines.
I am crafted of dimensions, mathematical, a prize.
I am somewhat alive. The pale horror of me plays
several minor characters from day to day, all of whom
are unhurried and deft. There is no rest for
the wicked. There is no
                              remembering the grand.
I take the hands that hurt me and mistake them
for my hands. Fragility is a must. It is my mind.

Brother to me. Trapeze to me. Half-loosened.
Half-glued. A taste as sweet. I cannot
fall away. I cannot go
                        as far as god.
The world is as lonely as the lost glove,
and it snows, and the cold invents a lullaby.
Inside, we are cold. The graveyards are howling.
The elegies we know by heart seem to wake in us
and will not abate
                        and soon are lectures
from the Valentines of our cradles. We, cradled by
the metamorphosis. We invent ourselves
to be ill. We grow still at the door to the void.
The powers that be only smile while we burn.
There is a gnaw in me
                        I cannot unhand. There is
a spire in me constructed of sons the womb once
built, constructed of nil when added to water,
a mixture embellishing, a mixture renounced. I am
a mixture now and my clothes billow and swell.
If I do not happen soon,
                        I will not happen at all.

Working with the Instrument

Kill in the wind what can't be killed
from the trees. Kill it from the grasses,
the stars. Kill it from that one place
where it thrives. Kill it raw. Kill it rain.
Kill it from the blades that gauze its strength.
Kill it one aim through the crosshairs.
Kill it a hanging. Kill it a rope. Kill it
a girl too fickle to understand. Kill it
a world, a snip of wheat. Kill it exposed eaves.
Allergy to fiberglass. Kill it nettle sting.
Kill it bed of nails. Kill it walking barefoot
on the coals. Kill the way it builds.
If it will not fill the glass, kill it half empty.
If it will not form the words, kill it mute.
Kill it dead. Kill it good. If it will not thrive,
kill it until you remember. Kill it in the best
of times. Kill it until it is gentle. Kill it
afloat. Kill it alone in the saltwater's soak.
Kill it burnt. Kill it cut. Kill it with the guts
you'll need to finish the job. Kill its inside
first. Pour it out. Kill it until the ribs are
stripped down. Kill it for days. Kill it
locked. Kill it signaling with the lantern
twice. Kill it farmland. Kill it noise. Kill it
a gathering storm, a throw of clay,
a splice of wool caught along the wire.
It will scatter once it knows.
It will run as fast, as far. It will know the fold
of the deer's heart in the face of the hunter.
It will know the clipped limbs of paper dolls.
Kill it until it tries to bargain. Until it hints
at surrender. Kill its engine. Kill its armor.
The hour is anger, is artifact, is over.
Kill its veins, those stalled ravines.

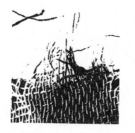

/

Dear B,

There is an arrow that is not my aim, making for the breast of the world. The left ventricle of my heart, at its odd angle, weeps. At birth, I am not born. The shepherd of my heart leaps among the yellow earth. There is no waking that is not my scream, branching like fire through the bone-dry woods, crying to be nested in the wind. And black death comes with its God cape. And black death comes with its godless mouth. A wafer of darkness will dissolve in the darkness. The rivers are names we say in our sleep. Insects drown out the moon. We live crouched down where an amen in the garden wakes. An amen in the heart's wall weeps. It was the wind that wounded us. It had our shape. It was the bloodhounds that smelled our hunger. Trade winds take us for a windowpane and turn. Death's black tackle in the harbor of the throat. Danger burns its lantern down our barley-darkened hold. Plait of the Lord, let me smolder.

Dear B,

This black trance where I lie like a cat, these arrows living naked in the after of my hands. Such resonance tempers the dark. I fever with impossibility. I fiddle with the antithesis of love. What lies in me is an armored starvation: I cringe at night. I go wild and pathological, schizophrenic as fire. The hiss you hear is my desire. I live on what exists before me, and I thrive. Nothing amounts to much. There are many of us, shaped brazen in the dark. Limbs bereft of significance. Visions within us weighing our hearts. Careless with the stampede in me, bleeding freely from the mouth, bellowing the anything down, risk takes my fingers delicately in its teeth. To kill me while I sleep. To sin differently. To kiss the hand of fate. Mute movements door my hands. Numb atoms dust my lovely death.

Dear B,

When I remake my life, I will let me lie, less slow with blooms. The dead
leaves rattle in their fascinated looks. There is no such lantern as the lakes
I spill. Reason is made of wishes. You asked if the light was too much. The
light is always too much. The light is walking toward something, don't you
think? I am finely etched. Visible. Delicate. Fractal as today languishes. Have
you seen the way it grows? The ajar night calls us to its potion banquet. God
save us from rigidity. God faint among the stars. When I find you, I am found,
when you shield me with what's vulnerable. This is enough in a world of
chasms. I don't hang from the nooses cellars are at night. Look at me. I float.

A Dictionary at the Turn of the Millennium

Hello to devouring, hello to digest,
to the end of lostness and the chill of less.
Hello to living like sardines.

To solace. To the offspring of hello.
Hello to desperation. Hello to welcome in.
Hello to generations that etcetera as we watch.

Hello to experiment with us.
Hello to angels at the mouth-ache
of more. Hello to the surgical morning.

Hello to the delicious red let of lakes,
to being gone like a long underwater.
Hello, it is an ordinary world, hello

limited time and autumn's pent-up monsters.
Hello, routine. Paralysis. Paradise.
Adrenaline catastrophe. Hello.

A Dictionary of Almost Drowning

The sea will go on migrating: four doves,
eight apostles, sedative and a September ecology.

The coming dusk is a granary, cross-stitching hallways
filled with gloom, with the throbbing coves turbines form.

You feed deep on such deadliness, its leeches like a sip
of water spilled on linen and skinned of inaudible selves.

They sidewind a throat through which you are spoken.

The sea goes on migrating. Moments named for years inhabit
its sleep. Hours briar like footprints to pin down its voice.

All the shops have closed their awnings, all their awnings
have gathered the last horizon's slackening reins.

All the headlights sequin late afternoon's pouting dress,
the peels like paper taken dry from an onion.

Isolation like a thin body against your own.

Your image dissolves in a sonograph of sorts,
as if you were an island and needed saving.

Already with roots elm-deep in you,
already a piñata where eleven railroads meet,

the sea will go on migrating. Knowing you will turn
as many times as there are knives in its swift machine.

A Dictionary of Limbo

I want to be anesthesia sly inside the patient,
counting down to knock her out.

I want to mount the mind's stallion and ride at last.
I want to fast while others feast.

I want to eat only what is tasteless.
I want to fake my death.

I want my enemies to love me,
I want to be remote.

I want my heart to seem a moat,
the water filled with fishes.

I want to wear night's crying
ricochet as a coat.

I want to be intent.
I want the details to relax.

I want to grow past rainfall measured
in inches. Grow useless in such

weather. Unable to relate.
A lapse of facets to face, a waste

of motley ends, a friend or enemy,
a violence called romance.

As if my metropolis had bloomed,
as if my old room were called new.

As if such global makings were a pseudonym
of my choice. With such muteness comes

a source—I have no voice—like the silicon
of mussel shells and the wedding bells' stung torque.

A Dictionary of Resignation

Enough. The dogs of god are loose.
Finally the nights you do not sleep
like packs outrun the wolves.

A wafer of darkness dissolves in the mouth,
as a language that has panted in the dirt.

The sky like the filter on a smoked cigarette.
Crows the smokestacks belch
to mar the possible, mineshaft days.

Touch is a rough crypt of covenants.
Random things awake.

Draft horses cart their owners to the grave.
The inept shall inherit the earth.

A Dictionary of Filming the Inside of a Tornado

—for Tim Samaras

1.

Unlid the sag, however late, the long collapse, unlid the weep,
let air in so the rush can breathe, let live, let tingle the capillary blood,
those tiny veins, unlid their sounds, sudden orchestra, dominant cells,
unlid the saints, their humble steps, their heads bowed wake us, spade in dirt,
unlid the stairs, the god, the sneeze, unlid the reasons not to look,
the early fate, an odd amount, as morning skins to paper kites,

unlid the plumes, the gentle coins, the quiet fields' unlively needs,
unlid generations, the violence made, unravel our weight from whatever bleeds,
the carrot seeds, unlid the thought, a small domestic crown of thorns,
unlid a temporary jealous tic, every lovely twist of snakes,
a blade the body beckons home, unlid its vases, noontime shriek,
years ago and not yet deep, a neckless bottle, sworn of cloud, unlid
to sleep sleep's darkened coat, as its rip reigns treason, unlid the hook.

2.

The pressure of air trembles
like a sentence in the mouth.

The land bows down to kiss the steel
that is the twist of cloud.

Clearings dream.
Seconds scatter.

The storm drains the void,
pours memory's trough.

The roofs howl, wrecked.
Farmers pray aloud.

The houses have poise
until they go down.

A Dictionary of Sun and Sea in the Voice of Icarus

This is not the world. It is only a pretty thing
with an astronomy of corpses. It is only rain
in the mouth like ash. Rain like an urn
for a thousand burned dead. Everything
swept clean. Dawn dressed in black, in a fabric
of singes. In oceans. A sabotage of weeds.

Sewn fast with this phosphorous of darlings,
my paradise bones know the mathematics
such savage waters sing. A mirage of churches
blooms. Returning is a dream I husk from
a field of years lost, has a labyrinth where
the groped wall unfolds too often. Empty
when its target is the jargon of my heart.

I mimic the sky to feel filled with terraces.
Sing a song for the dying and their launching
of ships, a mire of villages, the immaculate self.
Limbs to use as scaffolding for the sails that
take me south. Willows that long with their oceans
to be lost. Moments as lucid schisms. My thousand
hallucinations that weep a wailing undressed.

I want a body that hovers beyond equilibrium.
I am a blindness of water, housing epidemics:
if I have nothing else, I have fear. Obedient
and inched with sleep, stark with ribs
and lungs full of distance. Pieces agony
with light. Petticoats of amnesia dissolve.

Past dim fugitives that were my plummet,
my altered silhouette: backlit, my fingers trinket
like wind chimes along life's delicate trays.
Their animals resist domestication.
Stone feathers fall. I own their boroughs of salt.

A Dictionary in the Voice of Icarus

The wing is interrupted by a water made of trees.
Wing of straw. Wing of whispers. The wing is
interrupted by diamonds and the feathers

smile like a scar might, with a curve and many
facets, with a claw and beak and cry. The wing
outstretched is equal to a lantern. We solve

equations by its light. The wing has miles
of highway and travelers with bodies
like paper, with bodies like lichen or shell.

When chaos makes a mind it listens to,
the wing folds closed with a head beneath it.
All its furrows sleep. The wing has everything

I need, a season to happen for, a lick of seed,
a heavenly gray. The wing, the wing. Its underneath
cathedrals. Its colorlessness the neck of a lover

I have kissed, the way I have lain
beside someone, waiting, an explosion
in the heart's autumn leaves.

The wing has ten minutes to happen, to coal,
to omen, to slow us open, home with death.
The wing is an act of vanishing. The wing:

a mouth. A window we open to see the sky
crying October. To see the forests of ourselves
grow thin. Its jar filled with water is pain.

A Dictionary of Wandering and Homesickness
in the Voice of Odysseus

Home is the no I thought I knew before I'd mistaken it
for water. Its darks parch strangely in my roots.
Its gray sky grieves and is an opium for grieving.

Is a lullaby. Is very soft.
Bankrupts me of my bitter mouths.
Home is the lost veins singing.

Transcript of all time happening at once.
A hex of cold in the vestibule of it.
How low I have been is what it wants.

* * *

There is no home: there is only a future
where the cellos play and men bend their fragile heads
over old emotions. The eye is a journey
where the landscape becomes soft.

Lanterns answering the cities at night:
a great nostalgia. No strange absence
of streets. No dreaming teams of horses
to speak the waltz that never stops, its small boats

tethered by the cold-blooded stars.
The lunatic villages have in the wind's
small pocket young, electric girls.
The guards in the watchtower sleep.

A Dictionary Measuring Cause and Effect

Small bells tremble each antagonistic throat.
Wind is an opera torn seamless in the open;

its currents are a body permissive and displaced.
What begins breaks human bones.

Lipstick smear across the cheek,
vandal's scrawl beneath the bridge,

the glaze of a fountain noticeably chipped
by the bridles of drinking horses.

Wicks burned low until they burn out.
Railroads paraphrasing alternatives of silk.

A jig done by cattails in the heat
as they map the cartographer's hand.

The drift within an hour grows late.
The spin of this asymmetry casts a silhouette.

Please. Such accidents happen. Bitter flesh
is our bitter horse, working for its keep.

A Dictionary of Feigning Survival

Having altered the original,

cup rain in your luxury hands.

Drink from evening's ventriloquist baskets
what can't be coaxed from between its teeth.

Wind as the red inevitable.
Toxin-skinned. Semi-succulent.

Taste the salt that earns our keep.
Taste the laced-with river.

Do not love what you have driven away.

Come closer. Divorce your use.

A Dictionary of the Dead in the Voice of the Living Collective

They understand the scratch of roots at the ribless chest,
nights like a hum of water. Ropes eaten by rats.
Barbiturates acrid as wine. They denounce the self.

They bend as if willows were the masts of their ships,
their whispers softening rows of orchids. Their dark throats
like a prayer against the darkness. Iron in their voices

spills, bleeds a snapped branch or shoot.
They are magicians now that their hands
grow limp and their fingertips fill with scarves.

They think of flame but sing of ash, a drop
of this, a sip of that, their lairs inside us
skinned and mute. Eyes a snapshot of hunger.

A Dictionary of Perishing

I die alone. Rivers of my memory
parch. In each eye, a ruse of shadows.
Out my window, linen folds the moon.

My heart is a labyrinth of tendrils.
What takes me sounds wounded, what
takes me is soothed by the trees

as they shiver green ships onto
the pavement. Out my window, rain
personifies the consonants of day.

I become a small boat left to the current.
My hair a trail of ivy, my hair a wild
of carousels or the door to something

smoke. Yesterday sleeps infinite nights
in the same copper bed while I hold it
in my arms, my eclipse, while I touch

my wrists to the razors it wept.
An affliction that skins me at the mouth.
An insomnia no chemical could crack.

Shrouds grackle. Shallows mend.
I grow tired of the mire that dreams me
into less. I grow tired of waiting for the moment.

Bones, with their forever, shine. Soft
in a simile of ashes. Inside me, thresholds,
groves enough. Oblivion: the stem of any flower.

A Dictionary of the Afterlife

It tangles words, it swims armless with a limb
of cries and cuts and feeds on and soothes.
It is gathering hours it will soon use to feel,

it will morphine an entire world, it will turn
the earth to sticks and stones,
it will digest the bones to break them.

I cover it with leaves as though a cradle were its rind.
The boards of its eaves warp. Its blackbirds are wastrels.
It will not hatch. Its feathers will go old as cork.

I will drown it in the fountains I already think of
as here, great pines of snow growing from the fences,
chaos set against us like a pack of sorry dogs.

Its very disciples trail in my limbs: beachless,
the nightmares of children, the Rorschach of rain.
Better to quiet it now while the light's still thin.

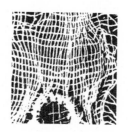

Dear B,

I knew it was a vision when I was killed and from my wound grew water. I knew it from the way my age gained speed. I was lost inside a place that looked familiar. A small moss at the altar. A splinter where I touched. When I went to find winter, I was born of the salt, I could only see my hands, I grew winded. I could only see my wrists. I grew like a forest, I knew me by my roots. I was on my knees and crying to be born. There was a gospel in my blood. Some things are impossible: I had already been sold to the world. Still there was a mystery, winter did not come. The way my pupils responded spoke volumes: they decided a window was a way of singing when they tried mixing laughter with a catastrophe of light. By listening, I was finally invented. I was the dog's long voice, buying back the evening's rattled coat of wings. I realized I was made of winter, and the will to carry on.

Notes

Page 39
Marion Parker was twelve years old in 1927 when she was
kidnapped, murdered, and dismembered.

Page 58
Tim Samaras was the first scientist to film the inside of a tornado.
He died chasing a storm in El Reno, Oklahoma, in 2013.

Acknowledgments

Grateful acknowledgment is made to the editors of the following journals, in which some of these poems first appeared:

Academy of American Poets *Poem-a-Day:* "Conspiracy to Commit Larceny: A Recipe."

American Poetry Review: "Corrosion Therapy" and "Criminal How-To."

Bellingham Review: "A Dictionary of Mechanics, Memory, and Skin in the Voice of Marion Parker."

Columbia, A Journal of Literature and Art: "A Dictionary of Feigning Survival" and "A Dictionary of Resignation."

Crazyhorse: "A Dictionary of the Garment" and "A Dictionary at the Turn of the Millennium."

Denver Quarterly: "Dear B, [I knew it was a vision]" and "Dear B, [Today, the rain is a dream]."

Fusion: "Dear B, [This black trance where I lie]" and "Dear B, [Two months of spasms]."

Green Mountains Review: "A Dictionary of Wandering and Homesickness in the Voice of Odysseus."

Hotel Amerika: "Dear B, [And my letter to you]," "Dear B, [The revision of need]," and "Dear B, [When I remake my life]."

Iowa Review: "A Dictionary of the Symphony in the Voice of Ludwig van Beethoven," "A Dictionary of What Can Be Learned in the Voice of the Sociopath's Lover," and "A Dictionary of Wooing and Deception in the Voice of the Sociopath."

The Journal: "Dear B, [There is an arrow that is not my aim]."

Kenyon Review: "A Dictionary of Preserving the Hydrangea's Bloom" and "A Dictionary in the Voice of Icarus."

Los Angeles Review: "A Dictionary of Following and Fading in the Voice of Eurydice."

Mid-American Review: "A Dictionary of Almost Drowning" and "A Dictionary of the Dead in the Voice of the Living Collective."

North American Review: "A Gospel of the Human Condition" and "A Letter to the Coroner in the Voice of Marion Parker."

The Paris-American: "A Dictionary at the Periphery" and "A Dictionary of Perishing."

Poetry London: "A Dictionary of Having Been Prey in the Voice of the Grandmother."

Spoon River Poetry Review: "A Dictionary of Sun and Sea in the Voice of Icarus."

Verse: "Conspiracy to Commit Larceny," "A Dictionary of the Afterlife," "A Dictionary of Faith," "A Dictionary of Filming the Inside of a Tornado," "A Dictionary of Keeping Quiet Between the Monstrous and Holy in the Voice of Marion Parker," "A Dictionary Measuring Cause and Effect," "Song of Interrogation," and "Working with the Instrument."

"A Dictionary at the Turn of the Millennium" is included in *Poet Showcase: An Anthology of New Hampshire Poets,* edited by Alice B. Fogel and Sidney Hall Jr. (Hobblebush Books, 2015).

"A Dictionary of Venery in the Voice of Artemis" was awarded the Barbara Bradley Award from the New England Poetry Club.

"A Dictionary of Mechanics, Memory, and Skin in the Voice of Marion Parker" was awarded the 49th Parallel Award from *Bellingham Review.*

"A Dictionary of Following and Fading in the Voice of Eurydice" was awarded the Ruskin Art Club Poetry Prize from Red Hen Press.

"A Dictionary of the Symphony in the Voice of Ludwig van Beethoven," "A Dictionary of What Can Be Learned in the Voice of the Sociopath's Lover," and "A Dictionary of Wooing and Deception in the Voice of the Sociopath" were named by Li-Young Lee as runner up for the *Iowa Review* Poetry Prize.

Thank you to Bronwyn Becker, Joelle Biele, B. K. Fischer, Jeff Friedman, Marie Gauthier, William Kuch, Jeffrey Levine, Tim Liardet, Jim Schley, Reginald Shepherd, and Harry Whitford (in memoriam) for their help in constructing this book.

Other books from Tupelo Press

Fasting for Ramadan: Notes from a Spiritual Practice (memoir), Kazim Ali
Another English: Anglophone Poems from Around the World (anthology),
    edited by Catherine Barnett and Tiphanie Yanique
Pulp Sonnets (poems, with drawings by Amin Mansouri), Tony Barnstone
gentlessness (poems), Dan Beachy-Quick
Everything Broken Up Dances (poems), James Byrne
One Hundred Hungers (poems), Lauren Camp
New Cathay: Contemporary Chinese Poetry (anthology), edited by Ming Di
Calazaza's Delicious Dereliction (poems), Suzanne Dracius,
    translated by Nancy Naomi Carlson
Gossip and Metaphysics: Russian Modernist Poetry and Prose (anthology),
    edited by Katie Farris, Ilya Kaminsky, and Valzhyna Mort
The Posthumous Affair (novel), James Friel
Entwined: Three Lyric Sequences (poems), Carol Frost
Poverty Creek Journal (lyric memoir), Thomas Gardner
The Good Dark (poems), Annie Guthrie
The Faulkes Chronicle (novel), David Huddle
Halve (poems), Kristina Jipson
Darktown Follies (poems), Amaud Jamaul Johnson
Dancing in Odessa (poems), Ilya Kaminsky
A God in the House: Poets Talk About Faith (interviews),
    edited by Ilya Kaminsky and Katherine Towler
Third Voice (poems), Ruth Ellen Kocher
Boat (poems), Christopher Merrill
Lucky Fish (poems), Aimee Nezhukumatathil
Weston's Unsent Letters to Modotti (poems), Chad Parmenter
Ex-Voto (poems), Adélia Prado, translated by Ellen Doré Watson
Mistaking Each Other for Ghosts (poems), Lawrence Raab
Intimate: An American Family Photo Album (hybrid memoir), Paisley Rekdal
Thrill-Bent (novel), *Jan Richman*
Cream of Kohlrabi (stories), Floyd Skloot
The Well Speaks of Its Own Poison (poems), Maggie Smith
The Perfect Life (lyric essays), Peter Stitt
Swallowing the Sea (essays), Lee Upton
Lantern Puzzle (poems), Ye Chun

See our complete list at www.tupelopress.org

/

CPSIA information can be obtained at www.ICGtesting.com
Printed in the USA
BVOW08s0754160416

444308BV00001B/3/P